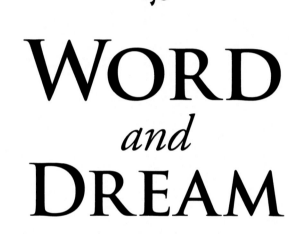

WORD
and
DREAM

ISMINI A. LYMPERI

AuthorHouse™ UK
1663 Liberty Drive
Bloomington, IN 47403 USA
www.authorhouse.co.uk
Phone: 0800.197.4150

Published by AuthorHouse 07/25/2018

ISBN: 978-1-5462-9568-6 (sc)
ISBN: 978-1-5462-9567-9 (e)

authorHOUSE®

Self-determined in the land of love,
where the forest
of oblivion and melancholy,
feeling to be
a breath before my crew
in that I dedicate…

...on my crew.

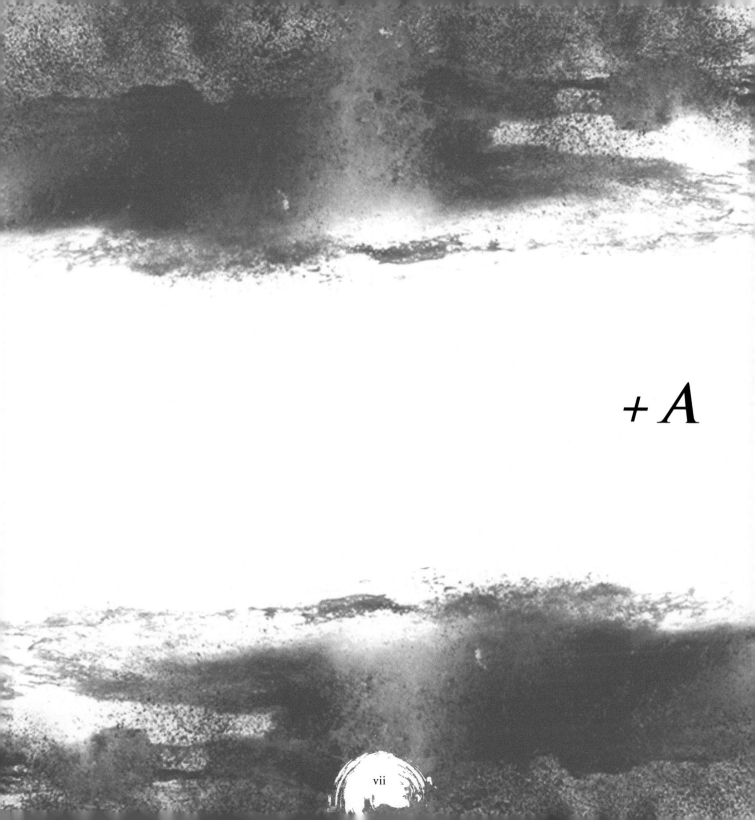

+*A*

Contents

Unsuccessful Efforts

1

Separation

Their silence is

all the love.

Their two hearts

an incombustible paper.

What can they expect

from their hearts

now that they have

become alone?

Hopeless Endeavors

White night…married with a voile.

In a sad mood, she is dancing on the musical stave of the soul

for the notes to roll on from the farewell that you said and left.

You just left.

You just stayed; I want them to become a blemish on my soul.

The body does not obey the dance of emotions which

vibrate loudly in the atmosphere.

A ring is not enough to fit our love.

It is a symbol of hopeless endeavors,

preserving the vanity that takes delight in the moments we

wait alone for each other.

The Myth and the Truth

The truth is in us,

and you are looking for it in matter… in a sacrifice that is not going to

be made by anyone for anyone.

Human life looks like a dream, with life being scattered

everywhere

only when you love me.

The myth of quest stays awake on the lips

and overwhelms us.

You know that the only truth is the quest of the myth,

and you keep on dragging up hopes and lost bodies

that were sacrificed—in vain—for what you are now willing

to sacrifice…

as long as you manage to discern the truth from the myth.

Why So Much Loneliness?

Yellow-orange autumn leaves

that took their last breaths

on the soil of my soul

when you left.

Drops of sorrow in the autumn landscape of my soul are hard

words; death is sweeter than my life.

What can words say when the silence of your absence is screaming?

You are lost…

Why did you erase the notes of the soul?

Why do you let me write about loneliness?

Why so much loneliness?

Loneliness

The frozen room will warm up the sorrow

of loneliness tonight.

Despair slaps me without mercy on the damp wall

of silence.

The shadow looks like a scarecrow… my loneliness, a grey meadow

on the hillside of life.

I have only courage left in me to turn off the light

in the dim room.

The sun sets behind the hillside,

and hope was lost with it.

The horizon went dark;

without Cerberus I may

not have discovered the way back.

Reflection Dance

In the Same Clearing

We both made it out to the same clearing.

Yes, this anticipation for the unknown sun that shone up

there and covered hope for the unexpected was sweet.

Who would expect our eyes would cover the darkness and our

bodies would illuminate the sorrow, stripping away the tension of the

moment… of this meeting of ours.

A pulse that beats forcefully in two bodies, love

beats in our chests… forcefully… as forcefully as it can.

The pulse is deafening… the sound…

In the notes we searched to find silence; the voices did not touch us…

the clarity of passion finally managed to blur thinking.

Light

My tears are a plea

for you to come back…

The whole world is one thousand problems

without the solutions.

I can see you standing away from me…

so cold.

Suddenly, the surroundings have become

full of light!

Way Out

Rain is falling.

The sun was hidden pale

behind the clouds.

You are looking out

of the window

for hope…

a little light.

Chasm

It is the silence

that beats me without mercy

over the walls of dejection.

My nerves,

spiderwebs

that wait patiently

to be separated by a wind

breaking inside me…

the gap of hope.

Reflection Dance

Serenity is a special moment tonight.

A candle of hope

will burn slowly to illuminate

our bodies,

painting shadows

that dance vividly

on the damp white walls.

Love Rain

Love Rain

White clouds,

yellow rain,

violet drops,

blue drops,

clear lust,

red thunder,

sight of the sun…

all of them nostalgic, on the wave.

Sunny love!

A Little and Not at All

A drop… of celestial scream,

A harbinger of rain.

A tear… of human error,

A harbinger of passion.

At any moment… close to him,

A harbinger of death.

Unrestrained Passion

Forceful passion,

flesh made of emotions,

a body throbbing with love.

A soul dancing

in the dark,

a heart beating

with somebody else's pulse.

Eyes imbued in mystery,

two worlds made of glass that die…

a few hermits who, as simple as that,

purely start wandering

over my body.

I live elusively

to see you

screaming passionately my name

and wondering

until when will you stand

this wandering about?

Where I Want to be Lost

The truth is clearly reflected

in your eyes tonight.

In the maze of your eyes

I would like to be lost,

to forget that I will die,

that I still live.

Figure

The sun rose

timidly

in the red storm

of my soul.

Your presence,

a sparkle

of unbound joy,

of stormy love.

What?

Could love be mania,

perhaps a rhapsody of passion?

Could it be a ray in the clouds,

a contagion of love in loneliness?

A touch of pain and pleasure,

a shiver to a scream?

Could a person in love,

with infinite emotion,

be a person saved?

Scream

21

Scream

A touch of death,

self-pity in silence;

a scream that leads to

the depths of sorrow

and loneliness.

Once more

alone in despair

of your chaotic scream.

You are the desert and the slow beats

of a heart that pulsates

not with blood but with the gall

of their indifference.

It's Been a Long Time

As my eyelids close

and look for hope in silence,

your figure

breaks the unfair silence.

It's been a long time that I haven't seen you,

and I feel like a shadow in Hades;

but like a figure, I bring you close,

and I slip out of the darkness.

The bitterness in my soul

will not find any comfort anymore.

Perhaps the tears will dry,

but you will be very far away then.

If my heart is not beating,

it is because you left.

Through the setting of my life,

the soul was painted grey.

Before the End

Before the End

An evil pirate

on the journey

of recollection.

A splash of thought

that is taken

to the end.

The agony of love

that is lost

in a sea of expectations.

A shipwreck of hope

with findings…

grey dreams.

Reflections

Tonight I thought of

erasing the moon

with a few clouds,

a piece of heaven.

Then I thought that

if I erase the moon,

I will find myself

without its light

in the emptiness.

You've Gone

It was not the coffee's fault,

the bitterness

that was left in my mouth…

on my lips.

It was the goodbye

kiss

that left its mark

tonight.

Lovers without Any Value

No… the dance of motives

of loveless lovers

is not affective.

No… the conception of the beauty of

lonely moments

is not inaccessible.

No… there is not any value.

Yes… there is not any value in

loveless moments of

lonely lovers.

Ismini A. Lymberi is a sociologist, staff nurse and student at the Medicine Faculty of Aristotle University of Thessaloniki. She has a master's of science in health promotion and health education from the Medicine Faculty of Athens and a master's of science in health management.

At the age of 12 she wrote her first poem titled 'The Battle of Salamis'. She felt wonderful when she heard the classmates' applause in the classroom. From that moment her pen followed the pulses of her heart.

She writes poems and essays and participates in Greek and international competitions. Her work has received praise and multiple awards.

- Praise during the International-Panhellenic Competition in the field of prose, Greece

- Piraeus Cultural Center 'FILON' 1988, Greece

- Diploma with medal in the 3rd International Literary Goncorso 'Giovanni Gronchi', Pontedera, Italy

- Diploma with medal in the 4th International Literary Goncorso 'Giovanni Gronchi', Pontedera, Italy

- Diploma with medal in the 5th International Literary Goncorso 'Roberto Bertelli', Pontedera, Italy

- 1st Prize in the category of Essay - Cultural Center of Piraeus 'O FILON', Greece

- Gold medal and progress excellence by the Ministry of Education and Religious Affairs of Greece

- XIII Goncorso Nazionale 'Franco Bargagna', Italy

- Praise for participation in the 3rd Greek Literary Narrative and Poetry Competition, Public Central Library of Chalkida, Greece

- Silver Stamp in the 18th Goncorso Nazionale 'Francgo Bargagna', Italy

- Diploma in parchment and participation with 3 poems in 'Antologia di fine millenio' Anthology of the 'Amici dell 'Umbria' organization for the year 2000, Italy

- Awards during the years 2006 - 2007 - 2008 at the International Competition 'Premio San Valentino', Italy

- 3rd Poetry Prize at the 2nd International - Greek Literature Contest of the Hellenic Spiritual Group of Cypriot Greece (HEPO), Greece

- Humanitarian Poetry Prize by the International Cultural Organization 'The Cafe of Ideas', in collaboration with the Municipality of Salamina, the UNESCO Club of Piraeus and Islands, the International Writers' Union and under the auspices of the Ministry of Culture, Greece

Books in the Field of Poetry:

- 'Skipfelis' editions I. Floros Athens 2000 - ISBN 9789607178558

- 'Word and Dream'- Printing House Panagiotis Papadopoulos Limnos 2007 in Greek Language

Printed in the United States
By Bookmasters